Edmond

A DRAMA

by David Mamet

S A M U E L F R E N C H , I N C.
45 West 25th Street   NEW YORK, N.Y. 10010
7623 Sunset Boulevard   HOLLYWOOD 90046
LONDON   *TORONTO*

To Richard Nelson and Wally Shawn

PROVINCETOWN PLAYHOUSE

The Goodman Theatre, The Provincetown Playhouse
David Jiranek, I. Michael Kasser, Marjorie Oberlander,
J.P. Pavanelli Limited and David Weil
present

EDMOND

by

DAVID MAMET

directed by

GREGORY MOSHER

with

PAUL BUTLER   RICK CLUCHEY   JOYCE HAZARD
LAURA INNES   BRUCE JARCHOW   LINDA KIMBROUGH
MARGE KOTLISKY   JOSÉ SANTANA
LIONEL MARK SMITH   COLIN STINTON   JACK WALLACE

Scenery by	Costumes by	Lighting by
BILL BARTELT	MARSHA KOWAL	KEVIN RIGDON

Fight Choreographer	General Manager	Stage Manager	Press Representatives
DAVID WOOLLEY	DAVID LAWLOR	KEN PORTER	SHIRLEY HERZ ASSOCIATES

Associate Producer Margot Harley

The world premiere of EDMOND was produced
by The Goodman Theatre, Chicago, Illinois.

4

The Setting:

NEW YORK CITY

THE CAST

(*in alphabetical order*)

A Mission Preacher, A Prisoner .... **PAUL BUTLER**

The Manager, A Leafleteer, A Customer, A Policeman, A Guard .... **RICK CLUCHEY**

A B-Girl, A Whore .... **JOYCE HAZARD**

A Peep Show Girl, Glenna .... **LAURA INNES**

A Man in a Bar, A Hotel Clerk, The Man in Back, A Chaplain .... **BRUCE JARCHOW**

Edmond's Wife .... **LINDA KIMBROUGH**

The Fortuneteller, A Manager, A Woman in the Subway .... **MARGE KOTLISKY**

A Cardsharp, A Guard .... **JOSÉ SANTANA**

A Shill, A Pimp .... **LIONEL MARK SMITH**

Edmond .... **COLIN STINTON**

A Bartender, A Bystander, A Pawnshop Owner, An Interrogator .... **JACK WALLACE**

The world premiere of EDMOND was produced by the Goodman Theatre, Chicago, Illinois, June 4, 1982 with the following cast:

PAUL BUTLER — A Mission Preacher, A Prisoner
RICK CLUCHEY — The Manager, A Leafleteer, A Customer, A Policeman, A Guard
JOYCE HAZARD — A B-Girl, A Whore
LAURA INNES — A Peep Show Girl, Glenna
BRUCE JARCHOW — A Man in a Bar, A Hotel Clerk, The Man in Back, A Chaplain
LINDA KIMBROUGH — Edmond's Wife
MARGE KOTLISKY — The Fortuneteller, A Manager, A Woman in the Subway
ERNEST PERRY, JR. — A Shill, A Pimp
JOSE SANTANA — A Cardsharp, A Guard
COLIN STINTON — Edmond
JACK WALLACE — A Bartender, A Bystander, A Pawnshop Owner, An Interrogator

This production was directed by Gregory Mosher; settings by Bill Bartelt; lighting by Kevin Rigdon; costumes by Marsha Kowal, fight choreography by David Woolley; stage manager, Tom Biscotto and Anne Clark.

The New York production opened at the Provincetown Playhouse on October 27, 1982 with Lionel Mark Smith playing the roles of A Shill, A Pimp.

Hokey Pokey Wicky Wamm
Salacapinkus Muley Comm
Tamsey Wamsey Wierey Wamm
King of the Cannibal Islands
                              Popular Song

THE CHARACTERS

FORTUNE-TELLER
EDMOND, a man in his late thirties.
HIS WIFE
A MAN IN A BAR
A B-GIRL
A BARTENDER
THE MANAGER
A PEEP-SHOW GIRL
THREE GAMBLERS
A CARD SHARP
A BYSTANDER
TWO WHILLS
A LEAFLETEER
A MANAGER (F)
A WHORE
A HOTEL CLERK
A PAWNSHOP OWNER
A CUSTOMER
THE MAN IN THE BACK
A WOMAN ON THE SUBWAY
A PIMP
GLENNA, a waitress
A MISSION PREACHER
A POLICEMAN
AN INTERROGATOR
A PRISONER
A CHAPLAIN
A GUARD

The Setting: New York City

IMPORTANT ADVERTISING
& BILLING REQUIREMENT

ALL producers of EDMOND must give credit to David Mamet as the author of the play in all programs distributed in connection with performances of the play, and in all instances in which the title of the play appears for advertising, publicizing or otherwise exploiting the play and/or production, including playbills, house-boards, throwaways, circulars, announcements, and whenever and wherever the title of the play appears.

The name of David Mamet shall be in size, type and prominence at least sixty five percent (65%) of the size of the type used for the title, and must appear immediately following the title of the play on a separate line upon which no other matter appears.

Edmond

SCENE 1

THE FORTUNE-TELLER

*EDMOND and the FORTUNE-TELLER seated across
the table from each other.*

FORTUNE-TELLER. If things are predetermined surely
they must manifest themselves. When we look back — as
we look back — we see that we could never have done
otherwise than as we did. (*pause*) Surely, then, there
must have been signs. If only we could have read them.
We say "I see now that I could not have done otherwise
. . . my *diet* caused me. Or my stars . . . which caused
me to eat what I ate . . . or my *genes,* or some other
thing beyond my control forced me to act as I did . . ."
And those things which *forced* us, of course, must make
their signs: our *diet,* or our *genes,* or our *stars.* (*pause*)
And there *are* signs. What we see reflects (more than
what is) what is to be. (*pause*) Are you cold?

EDMOND. No. (*pause*)

FORTUNE-TELLER. Would you like me to close the
window?

EDMOND. No, thank you.

FORTUNE-TELLER. Give me your palm. (*EDMOND
does so.*) You are not where you belong. It is perhaps
true none of us are, but in your case this is more true
than in most. We all like to believe we are special. In
your case this is true. Listen to me: (*She continues talk-*

11

ing as the lights dim.) The world seems to be crumbling around us. You look and you wonder if what you perceive is accurate. And you are unsure what your place is. To what extent you are cause and to what an effect . . .

SCENE 2

AT HOME

EDMOND and his WIFE are sitting in the livingroom. A pause.

WIFE. The girl broke the lamp. (*pause*)
EDMOND. Which lamp?
WIFE. The antique lamp.
EDMOND. In my room?
WIFE. Yes. (*pause*)
EDMOND. Huh.
WIFE. That lamp cost over two hundred and twenty dollars.
EDMOND. (*pause*) Maybe we can get it fixed.
WIFE. We're never going to get it fixed, I think that that's the *point* . . . I think that's why she did it.
EDMOND. Yes. Alright—I'm going. (*Pause. He gets up and starts out of the room.*)
WIFE. Will you bring me back some cigarettes . . .
EDMOND. I'm not coming back.
WIFE. What?
EDMOND. I'm not coming back. (*pause*)
WIFE. What do you mean?
EDMOND. I'm going, and I'm not going to come back. (*pause*)
WIFE. You're not *ever* coming back?

EDMOND. No.

WIFE. Why not? (*pause*)

EDMOND. I don't want to live this kind of life.

WIFE. What does that mean?

EDMOND. That I can't live this life.

WIFE. "You can't live this life" so you're leaving me?

EDMOND. Yes.

WIFE. Ah. Ah. Ah. And what about "ME?" Don't you *love* me any more?

EDMOND. No.

WIFE. You don't?

EDMOND. No.

WIFE. And why is that?

EDMOND. I don't know.

WIFE. And when did you find this out?

EDMOND. A long time ago.

WIFE. You did?

EDMOND. Yes.

WIFE. How long ago?

EDMOND. Years ago.

WIFE. You've known for years that you don't love me?

EDMOND. Yes. (*pause*)

WIFE. Oh. (*pause*) Then why do you decide you're leaving *now?*

EDMOND. I've had enough.

WIFE. Yes. But why *now?*

EDMOND. (*pause*) Because you don't interest me spiritually or sexually. (*pause*)

WIFE. Hadn't you known this for some time?

EDMOND. What do you think?

WIFE. I think you did.

EDMOND. Yes, I did.

WIFE. And why didn't you leave then? Why didn't

you leave *then,* you stupid *shit!!!* All of these years you
say that you've been living here. . . ? (*pause*) Eh? You
idiot . . . *I've* had enough. You idiot . . . to see you
passing *judgement* on me all this time . . .

EDMOND. . . . . I never judged you . . .

WIFE. . . . and then you tell me. "You're leaving."

EDMOND. Yes.

WIFE. *Go,* then . . .

EDMOND. I'll call you.

WIFE. Please. And we'll talk. What shall we do with
the house? Cut it in half? Go. Get out of here. Go.

EDMOND. You think that I'm fooling.

WIFE. I do *not.* Goodbye. Thank you. Goodbye.
(*pause*) Goodbye. Get *out.* Get *out* of here. And don't
you *ever* come back. Do you hear me? (*exits, closing the
door on him*)

SCENE 3

AT A BAR

*EDMOND is at the bar. A MAN is next to him. They sit
for a while.*

MAN. . . . . I tell you who's got it *easy* . . .

EDMOND. Who?

MAN. The niggers. (*pause*) Sometimes I wish I was a
nigger.

EDMOND. Sometimes I do, too.

MAN. I'd rob a store. I don't blame them. I swear to
God. Because I want to tell you: we're *bred* to do the
things that we do.

EDMOND. Mm.

MAN. Northern Race *one* thing, and the Southern
Race something else. And what *they* want to do is sit

beneath the tree and watch the elephant. (*pause*) And I don't blame them one small bit. Because there's too much *pressure* on us.

EDMOND. Yes.

MAN. And that's no joke, and that's not *poetry*, it's just too much.

EDMOND. It is. It absolutely is.

MAN. A man's got to get *out* . . .

EDMOND. What do you mean?

MAN. A man's got to get *away* from himself . . .

EDMOND. . . . that's true . . .

MAN. . . . because the pressure is too much.

EDMOND. What do you do?

MAN. What do you mean?

EDMOND. What do you do to get out?

MAN. What do I do?

EDMOND. Yes.

MAN. What are the things to do? What are the things *anyone* does. . . ? (*pause*) *Pussy* . . . I don't know . . . *Pussy* . . . *Power* . . . *Money* . . . uh, . . . *adventure* . . . (*pause*) I think that's it . . . uh, self-*destruction* . . . I think that that's it . . . don't you. . . ?

EDMOND. Yes.

MAN. . . . uh, *religion* . . . I suppose that's it, uh, *release,* uh, ratification. (*pause*) You have to get *out,* you have to get something opens your *nose,* life is too *short.*

EDMOND. My wife and I are incompatible.

MAN. I'm sorry to hear that. (*pause*) In what way?

EDMOND. I don't find her attractive.

MAN. Uh huh . . .

EDMOND. . . . and she hates my guts.

MAN. Mm.

EDMOND. It's a boring thing to talk about. But that's what's on my mind.

MAN. I understand.

EDMOND. You do?

MAN. Yes. (*pause*)

EDMOND. Thank you.

MAN. Believe me, that's alright. I know that we all *need* it, and we don't know where to *get* it, and I know what it *means,* and I understand.

EDMOND. . . . I feel . . .

MAN. I know. Like your balls were cut off.

EDMOND. Yes. A long, long time ago.

MAN. Mm. Hm.

EDMOND. And I don't feel like a man.

MAN. Do you know what you need?

EDMOND. No.

MAN. You need to get laid.

EDMOND. I do. I know I do.

MAN. That's why the niggers have it easy.

EDMOND. Why?

MAN. I'll tell you why: there are responsibilities they never have accepted. (*pause*) Try the "Allegro."

EDMOND. What is that?

MAN. A bar on 47th street.

EDMOND. Thank you. (*The MAN gets up, pays for drinks.*)

MAN. I want this to be on me. I want you to *remember* there was someone who listened. (*pause*) You'd do the same for me. (*The MAN exits.*)

SCENE 4

THE ALLEGRO

EDMOND sits by himself for a minute. A B-GIRL comes by.

B-GIRL. You want to buy me a drink?

EDMOND. Yes. (*pause*) I'm putting myself at your *mercy* . . . this is my first time in a place like this. I don't want to be taken advantage of. (*pause*) You understand?

B-GIRL. Buy me a drink and we'll go in the back.

EDMOND. And do what?

B-GIRL. Whatever you want. (*EDMOND leans over and whispers to B-GIRL.*) Ten dollars.

EDMOND. Alright.

B-GIRL. Buy me a drink.

EDMOND. You get a commission on the drinks?

B-GIRL. Yes. (*She gestures to BARTENDER who brings drinks.*)

EDMOND. How much commission do you get?

B-GIRL. Fifty percent.

BARTENDER. (*bringing drinks*) That's twenty bucks.

EDMOND. (*getting up*) It's too much.

BARTENDER. What?

EDMOND. Too much. Thank you.

B-GIRL. Ten!

EDMOND. No, thank you.

B-GIRL. Ten!

EDMOND. I'll give you five. I'll give you the five you'd get for the drink if I gave them ten. But I'm not going to give them ten.

B-GIRL. But you have to buy me a drink.

EDMOND. I'm sorry. No.

B-GIRL. Alright. (*pause*) Give me ten.

EDMOND. On top of the ten?

B-GIRL. Yeah. You give me twenty.

EDMOND. I should give you twenty.

B-GIRL. Yes.

EDMOND. To *you*.

B-GIRL. Yes.

EDMOND. And then you give him the five?

B-GIRL. Yes. I got to give him the five.

EDMOND. No.

B-GIRL. For the *drink*.

EDMOND. No. You don't have to pay him for the drink. It's *tea* . . .

B-GIRL. It's not tea.

EDMOND. It's not tea! . . . ? (*He drinks.*) If it's not *tea* what *is* it, then. . . ? I came here to be *straight* with you, why do we have to go through this. . . ?

MANAGER. Get in or get out. (*pause*) Don't mill around. Get in or get out . . . (*pause*) Alright. (*MANAGER escorts EDMOND out of the bar.*)

SCENE 5

A PEEP SHOW

Booths with closed doors all around. A GIRL in a spangled leotard sees EDMOND and motions him to a booth whose door she is opening.

GIRL. Seven. Go in Seven. (*He starts to Booth Seven.*) No. Six! I mean Six. Go in Six. (*He goes into Booth Six. She disappears behind the row of booths, and appears behind a plexiglass partition in Booth Six.*) Take your dick out. (*pause*) Take your dick out. (*pause*) Come on. Take your dick out.

EDMOND. I'm not a cop.

GIRL. I know you're not a cop. Take your dick out. I'm gonna give you a good time.

EDMOND. How can we get this barrier to come down?

GIRL. It doesn't come down.

EDMOND. Then how are you going to give me a good time?

GIRL. Come here. (*He leans close. She whispers.*) Give me ten bucks. (*pause*) Give me ten bucks. (*pause*) Put it through the thing. (*She indicates a small ventilator hole in the plexiglass. Pause.*) Put it through the thing.

EDMOND. (*checking his wallet*) I haven't got ten bucks.

GIRL. Okay . . . just . . . yes. Okay. Give me the twenty.

EDMOND. Are you going to make me change?

GIRL. Yes. Just give me the twenty. Give it to me. Good. Now take your dick out.

EDMOND. Can I have my ten?

GIRL. Look let me hold the ten.

EDMOND. Give me the ten back. (*pause*) Come on. Give me my ten back.

GIRL. Let me hold the ten . . .

EDMOND. Give me my ten back and I'll give you a tip when you're done. (*Pause. She does so.*) Thank you.

GIRL. Okay. Take your dick out.

EDMOND. (*of the plexiglass*) How does this thing come down?

GIRL. It doesn't come down.

EDMOND. It doesn't come down?

GIRL. No.

EDMOND. Then what the fuck am I giving you ten bucks for?

GIRL. Look: you can touch me. Stick your finger in this you can touch me.

EDMOND. I don't want to touch *you* . . . I want *you* to touch *me* . . .

GIRL. I can't. (*pause*) I would, but I can't. We'd have

the cops in here. We would. Honestly. (*pause*) Look:
put your finger in here . . . come on. (*pause*) Come on.
(*He zips up his pants and leaves the booth.*) You're only
cheating your*self* . . .

SCENE 6

ON THE STREET. THREE CARD MONTE

A CARDSHARP, a BYSTANDER and Two SHILLS.

SHARPER. You pick the red you win, and twenty get
you forty. Put your money up. The *black* gets *back,* the
red you go ahead . . . Who saw the red. . . ? Who saw
the red? Who saw her. . . ?

BYSTANDER. (*to EDMOND*) The fellow over there is
a shill . . .

EDMOND. Who is. . . ?

BYSTANDER. (*points*) You want to know how to beat
the game?

EDMOND. How?

BYSTANDER. You figure out which card has got to
win . . .

EDMOND. Uh huh . . .

BYSTANDER. . . . and bet the *other* one . . .

SHARPER. Who saw the red. . . ?

BYSTANDER. They're all shills, they're all part of an
act.

SHARPER. Who saw her? Five will get you ten . . .

SHILL. (*playing lookout*) Cops . . . cops . . . cops
. . . don't run . . . *don't* run . . . (*Everyone scatters.
Edmond moves down the street.*)

SCENE 7

PASSING OUT LEAFLETS

EDMOND moves down the street. A man is passing out leaflets.

LEAFLETEER. Check it out . . . check it out . . . This is what you looking for . . . Take it . . . I'm *giving* you something . . . *Take* it . . . (*EDMOND takes leaflet.*) Now: is that what you looking for or not. . . ?

EDMOND. (*reading leaflet*) Is this true. . . ?

LEAFLETEER. Would I give it to you if it wasn't. . . ? (*EDMOND walks off reading the leaflet. The LEAF-LETEER continues with his spiel.*) Check it out . . .

SCENE 8

THE WHOREHOUSE

EDMOND shows up with the leaflet. He talks to the MANAGER, a woman.

MANAGER. Hello.

EDMOND. Hello.

MANAGER. Have you been here before?

EDMOND. No.

MANAGER. How'd you hear about us? (*EDMOND shows her the leaflet.*) You from out-of-town?

EDMOND. Yes. What's the deal here?

MANAGER. This is a *health* club.

EDMOND. . . . . I know.

MANAGER. And our rates are by the hour. (*pause*)

EDMOND. Yes?

MANAGER. Sixty-eight dollars for the first hour, sauna, free bar, showers . . . (*pause*) The hour doesn't start until you and the masseuse are in the room.

EDMOND. Alright.

MANAGER. Whatever happens in the room, of course, is between you.

EDMOND. I understand.

MANAGER. You understand?

EDMOND. Yes.

MANAGER. . . . or, for two hours it's one hundred fifty dollars. If you want two hostesses that is two hundred dollars for one hour. (*pause*) Whatever arrangement that you choose to *make* with them is between *you*.

EDMOND. Good. (*pause*)

MANAGER. What would you like?

EDMOND. One hour.

MANAGER. You pay that now. How would you like to pay?

EDMOND. How can I pay?

MANAGER. With cash or credit card. The billing for the card will read "Atlantic Ski and Tennis."

EDMOND. I'll pay you with cash.

SCENE 9

UPSTAIRS AT THE WHOREHOUSE

EDMOND and the WHORE are in a cubicle.

WHORE. How are you?

EDMOND. Fine. I've never done this before.

WHORE. No? (*She starts rubbing his neck.*)

EDMOND. No. That feels very good. (*pause*)

WHORE. You've got a good body.

EDMOND. Thank you.

WHORE. Do you work out? (*pause*)

EDMOND. I jog.

WHORE. Mmm. (*pause*)

EDMOND. And I use to play football in high school.

WHORE. You've kept yourself in good shape.

EDMOND. Thank you.

WHORE. (*pause*) What shall we do?

EDMOND. I'd like to have intercourse with you.

WHORE. That sounds very nice. I'd like that too.

EDMOND. You would?

WHORE. Yes.

EDMOND. How much would that be?

WHORE. For a straight fuck that would be a hundred fifty.

EDMOND. That's too much.

WHORE. You know that I'm giving you a break . . .

EDMOND. . . . no . . .

WHORE. Because this is your first time here . . .

EDMOND. No. It's too much, on top of the sixty-eight at the door . . .

WHORE. . . . I know. I know, but you know, I don't get to keep it all. I *split* with them. Yes. They don't pay me, I pay *them*.

EDMOND. It's too much. (*pause. The WHORE sighs.*)

WHORE. How much do you have?

EDMOND. All I had was one hundred for the whole thing.

WHORE. You mean a hundred for it all.

EDMOND. That only left me thirty.

WHORE. Nooo, honey, you couldn't get a *thing* for that.

EDMOND. Well, how much do you want?

WHORE. (*sighs*) Alright, for a straight fuck, one hundred twenty.

EDMOND. I couldn't pay that.

WHORE. I'm sorry, then. It would have been nice.

EDMOND. I'll give you eighty.

WHORE. No.

EDMOND. One hundred.

WHORE. Alright, but only, you know cause this is your first time.

EDMOND. I know.

WHORE. . . . cause we *split* with them, you understand . . .

EDMOND. I understand.

WHORE. Alright. One hundred.

EDMOND. Thank you. I appreciate this. (*pause*) Would it offend you if I wore a rubber. . . ?

WHORE. Not at all. (*pause*)

EDMOND. Do you have one. . . ?

WHORE. Yes. (*pause*) You want to pay me now. . . ?

EDMOND. Yes. Certainly. (*He takes out his wallet. Hands her a credit card.*)

WHORE. I need cash, honey.

EDMOND. They said at the door I pay with my . . .

WHORE. That was at the door . . . you have to *pay* me with *cash* . . .

EDMOND. I don't think I *have* it . . . (*He checks through his wallet.*) I don't *have* it . . .

WHORE. How much do you have. . . ?

EDMOND. I, uh, only have *sixty*.

WHORE. Jeez, I'm *sorry* honey, but I can't *do* it . . .

EDMOND. Well, wait, wait, wait, wait, maybe we could . . . wait . . .

WHORE. Why don't you *get* it, and come *back* here . . .

EDMOND. Well, where could I *get* it. . . ?

WHORE. Go to a restaurant and cash a check, I'll be here til *four* . . .

EDMOND. I'll. I'll . . . um, um, . . . *yes. Thank* you . . .

WHORE. Not at all. (*EDMOND leaves the whorehouse.*)

SCENE 10

THREE CARD MONTE

EDMOND out on the street, passes by the three-card-monte men, who have assembled again.

SHARPER. You can't win if you don't play . . . (*to EDMOND*) *You* sir . . .

EDMOND. Me. . . ?

SHARPER. You going to try me again. . . ?

EDMOND. Again. . . ?

SHARPER. *I* remember you beat me out of that *fifty* that time with your girlfriend . . .

EDMOND. . . . when was this?

SHARPER. On four*teenth* street . . . you going to try me one more time. . . ?

EDMOND. Uh . . .

SHARPER. . . . play you for that fifty . . . fifty get you one hundred, we see you as fast as you was . . . Pay on the red, pass on the black . . . where is the queen . . . you pick the queen you win . . . *where* is the queen . . . who saw the queen . . . You put up fifty win a hundred . . . Now: Who saw the queen. . . ?

SHILL. I got her!

SHARPER. How much? Put your money up. How much?

SHILL. I bet you fifty dollars.

SHARPER. Put it up. (*The SHILL does so. The SHILL turns a card.*)

SHILL. There!

SHARPER. My man, I'm jus' too quick for you today. *Who* saw the queen. We got two cards left. Pay on the *red* queen, who saw her?

EDMOND. I saw her.

SHARPER. Ah, *shit,* man, you too fass for me.

EDMOND. . . . for fifty dollars . . .

SHARPER. All right—all right. Put it up. (*pause*)

EDMOND. Will you pay me if I win?

SHARPER. Yes I will. If you win. But you got to *win* first . . .

EDMOND. All that I've got to do is turn the queen.

SHARPER. Thass all you got to do.

EDMOND. I'll bet you fifty.

SHARPER. You sure?

EDMOND. Yes. I'm sure.

SHARPER. Put it up. (*EDMOND does so.*) Now: which one you like?

EDMOND. (*turning card*) There!

SHARPER. (*taking money*) I'm *sorry,* my man. This time you lose—now we even. Take another shot. You pick the queen you win . . . bet you another fifty . . .

EDMOND. Let me see those cards.

SHARPER. These cards are fine, it's you thass slow.

EDMOND. I want to see those cards.

SHARPER. These cards are good, my man, you *lost*.

EDMOND. You let me see those cards.

SHARPER. You ain't goin' *see* no motherfuckin cards, we playing a *game* here . . .

SHILL. . . . you lost, *get* lost.

EDMOND. Give me those cards, fella.

SHARPER. You want to see the cards? You want to see cards. . . ? *Here* is the motherfuckin cards . . . (*He hits EDMOND in the face. He and the SHILL beat EDMOND for several seconds, EDMOND falls to the ground.*)

SCENE 11

A HOTEL

EDMOND, torn and battered, comes up to the desk CLERK.

EDMOND. I want a room.

CLERK. Twenty-two dollars. (*pause*)

EDMOND. I lost my wallet.

CLERK. Go to the police.

EDMOND. You can call up American Express.

CLERK. Go to the police. (*pause*) I don't want to hear it.

EDMOND. You can call the credit-card people. I have insurance.

CLERK. Call them yourself. Right across the hall.

EDMOND. I have no money.

CLERK. I'm sure it's a free call.

EDMOND. Do those phones require a dime?

CLERK. (*pause*) I'm sure I don't know.

EDMOND. You know if they need a *dime* or not. To get a *dial* tone . . . You know if they need a *dime,* for chrissake. Do you want to live in that kind of world? Do you want to live in a *world* like that? I've been *hurt*. Are you *blind?* Would you appreciate it if I acted this way to *you?* (*pause*) I *asked* you one simple thing. Do they need a *dime.*

CLERK. No. They don't need a dime. You make your call, and you go somewhere else.

SCENE 12

THE PAWNSHOP

The OWNER waiting on a CUSTOMER.

CUSTOMER. Whaddaya get for that? What is that? Fourteen or eighteen?

OWNER. Fourteen.

CUSTOMER. Yeah? Lemme see that. How much is that?

OWNER. Six hundred eighty-five.

CUSTOMER. Why is that? How old is that? Is that *old?*

OWNER. You know how much *gold* that you got in there? Feel. That. Just feel that.

CUSTOMER. Where is it marked?

OWNER. Right there. You want that loupe?

CUSTOMER. No . . . I can see it.

(*EDMOND comes into the store and stands by the two.*)

OWNER. (*to EDMOND*) What?

EDMOND. I want to pawn something.

OWNER. Talk to the man in back.

CUSTOMER. What else you got like this?

OWNER. I don't know *what* I got. You're *looking* at it.

CUSTOMER. (*pointing to item in display case*) Lemme see that.

EDMOND. (*goes to man in back behind grate*) I want to pawn something.

MAN. What?

EDMOND. My ring. (*holds up hand*)

MAN. Take it off.

EDMOND. It's difficult to take it off.

MAN. Spit on it. (*EDMOND does so.*)

CUSTOMER. How much is that?

OWNER. Two hundred twenty.

EDMOND. (*happily*) I got it off. (*EDMOND hands the ring to the man.*)

MAN. What do you want to do with this? You want to pawn it?

EDMOND. Yes. How does that work?

MAN. Is that what you want to do?

EDMOND. Yes. Are there other things to do?

MAN. . . . what you can *do,* no, I mean, if you wanted it *appraised* . . .

EDMOND. Uh huh . . .

MAN. . . . or want to *sell* it . . .

EDMOND. Uh huh . . .

MAN. . . . or you wanted it to *pawn* . . .

EDMOND. I understand.

MAN. Alright?

EDMOND. How much is getting it appraised?

MAN. Five dollars.

CUSTOMER. Lemme see something in black.

EDMOND. What would you give me if I pawned it?

MAN. What do you want for it?

EDMOND. What is it worth?

MAN. You pawn it all you're gonna get's approximately . . . you know how this works?

CUSTOMER. Yes. Let me see that . . .

EDMOND. No.

MAN. What you get, a quarter of the value.

EDMOND. Mm.

MAN. Approximately. For a year. You're paying twelve per-cent. You can redeem your pledge with the year you pay your twelve per-cent. To that time. Plus the amount of the loan.

EDMOND. What is my pledge?

MAN. Well, that depends on what it *is*.

EDMOND. What do you mean?

MAN. What it *is*. Do you understand?

EDMOND. No.

MAN. Whatever the amount *is*, that is your pledge.

EDMOND. The amount of the loan.

MAN. That's right.

EDMOND. I understand.

MAN. Alright. What are you looking for, the ring?

CUSTOMER. Nope. Not today. I'll catch you next time. Lemme see that knife.

EDMOND. What is it worth?

MAN. The most I can give you, hundred twenty bucks.

CUSTOMER. This is nice.

EDMOND. I'll take it.

MAN. Good. I'll be right back. Give me the ring. (*ED-MOND does so. EDMOND wanders over to watch the other transaction.*)

CUSTOMER. (*holding up knife*) What are you asking for this?

OWNER. Twenty-three bucks. Say, twenty bucks.

CUSTOMER. (*to himself*) Twenty bucks . . .

EDMOND. Why is it so expensive?

OWNER. Why is it so expensive?

CUSTOMER. No. I'm going to pass. (*hands knife back, exiting*) I'll catch you later.

OWNER. Right.

EDMOND. Why is the knife so expensive?

OWNER. This is a *survival* knife. G.I. Issue. World War Two. And that is why.

EDMOND. Survival knife.

OWNER. That is correct.

EDMOND. Is it a good knife?

OWNER. It is the best knife that money can buy. (*He starts to put the knife away. As an afterthought.*) You want it?

EDMOND. Let me think about it for a moment.

SCENE 13

THE SUBWAY

EDMOND is in the subway. Waiting with him, is a WOMAN in a hat.

EDMOND. (*pause*) My mother had a hat like that. (*pause*) My mother had a hat like that. (*pause*) I . . . I'm not making conversation. She wore it for years. She had it when I was a child. (*The WOMAN starts to walk away. EDMOND grabs her.*) I wasn't just making it "up". It *happened* . . .

WOMAN. (*detaching herself from his grip*) Excuse me . . .

EDMOND. . . . who the fuck do you think you *are*. . . ? I'm *talk*ing to you . . . what am I? A *stone*. . . ? Did I say, "I want to lick your pussy. . . ?" I said, "My mother had that same hat . . ." You *cunt* . . . What am

I? A *dog?* I'd like to slash your fucking *face* . . . I'd like to slash your motherfucking *face* apart . . .

WOMAN. . . . WILL SOMEBODY *HELP* ME . . .

EDMOND. *You* don't know who I am . . . (*She breaks free.*) Is everybody in this town *insane.* . . ? Fuck you . . . fuck you . . . fuck you . . . fuck the *lot* of you . . . fuck you *all* . . . I don't *need* you . . . I worked all of my life . . .

SCENE 14

ON THE STREET, OUTSIDE THE PEEP SHOW

PIMP. What are you looking for?

EDMOND. What?

PIMP. What are you looking for?

EDMOND. I'm not looking for a goddamn thing.

PIMP. You looking for that *joint,* it's *close.*

EDMOND. What joint?

PIMP. That *joint* that you was looking for.

EDMOND. Thank you, no. I'm not looking for that joint.

PIMP. You looking for *something,* and I think that I know what you looking for.

EDMOND. You do?

PIMP. You come with me I get you what you want.

EDMOND. What do I want?

PIMP. *I* know. We get you some *action,* my friend. We get you something sweet to shoot on. (*pause*) I know. Thass what I'm doing here.

EDMOND. What are you saying?

PIMP. I'm saying that we going to find you something nice.

EDMOND. You're saying that you're going to find me a woman.

PIMP. Thass what I'm *doing* out here, friend.

EDMOND. How much?

PIMP. Well, how much do you want?

EDMOND. I want somebody clean.

PIMP. Thass right.

EDMOND. I want a blowjob.

PIMP. Alright.

EDMOND. How much?

PIMP. Thirty bucks.

EDMOND. That's too much.

PIMP. How much do you want to *spen* . . .

EDMOND. Say fifteen dollars.

PIMP. Twenny five.

EDMOND. No. Twenty.

PIMP. Yes.

EDMOND. Is that alright?

PIMP. Give me the twenty.

EDMOND. I'll give it to you when we see the girl.

PIMP. Hey, I'm not going to *leave* you, man, you coming with me. We *goin* to see the girl.

EDMOND. Good. I'll give it to you then.

PIMP. You give it to me *now,* you unnerstan? Huh? (*pause*) Thass the trans*action.* (*pause*) You see? Unless you were a *cop.* (*pause*) You give me the money, and then thass en*trap*ment. (*pause*) You understand?

EDMOND. Yes. I'm not a cop.

PIMP. Alright.

PIMP. Do you *see* what I'm saying?

EDMOND. I'm sorry.

PIMP. Thass alright. (*EDMOND takes out wallet. Exchange of money.*) You come with me. Now we'll just walk here like we're talking.

EDMOND. Is she going to be clean?

PIMP. Yes, she is. I understand you, man. (*Pause. They walk.*) I understand what you want. (*pause*) Believe me. (*pause*)

EDMOND. Is there any money in this?

PIMP. Well, you know, man, there's *some* . . . you get done piecing off the *police,* this man *here* . . . the *medical,* the *bills,* you *know.*

EDMOND. How much does the girl get?

PIMP. Sixty percent.

EDMOND. Mm.

PIMP. *Oh* yeah. (*He indicates a spot.*) Up here. (*They walk to the spot. The PIMP takes out a knife and holds it to EDMOND's neck.*) Now give me all you money mothafucka! *Now!*

EDMOND. Alright.

PIMP. *All* of it. Don't turn around . . . don't turn aroun' . . . just put it in my hand.

EDMOND. Alright.

PIMP. . . . and don't you make a motherfuckin' sound . . .

EDMOND. I'm going to do everything you say . . .

PIMP. Now you just han' me all you got. (*EDMOND turns, strikes the PIMP in the face.*)

EDMOND. YOU MOTHERFUCKING NIGGER!

PIMP. Hold on . . .

EDMOND. You motherfucking *shit* . . . you *jungle* bunny . . . (*He strikes the PIMP again. He drops his knife.*)

PIMP. I . . .

EDMOND. You *coon,* you *cunt,* you *cock*sucker . . .

PIMP. I . . .

EDMOND. "Take me upstairs. . . ???"

PIMP. Oh, my god . . . (*The PIMP has fallen to the sidewalk and EDMOND is kicking him.*)

EDMOND. You *fuck*. You *nigger*. You dumb *cunt* . . .
You *shit* . . . You shit . . . (*pause*) You fucking *nigger*.
(*pause*) Don't fuck with *me*, you *coon* . . . (*pause. ED-
MOND spits on him.*) I hope you're *dead*. (*pause*)

SCENE 15

THE COFFEEHOUSE

*EDMOND swaggers into the coffeehouse and addresses
    the waitress, GLENNA.*

EDMOND. I want a cup of coffee. No a beer. Beer
chaser. Irish whiskey.
GLENNA. Irish whiskey.
EDMOND. Yes. A double. Huh.
GLENNA. You're in a peppy mood today.
EDMOND. You're godam right I am, and you want me
to tell you *why?* Because I am *alive.* You know how
much of our life we're alive, you and me? *Nothing.* Two
minutes out of the year. When we meet someone new,
when we get *married,* when, when, when, when we're in
difficulties . . . *once* in our life at the death of someone
that we love. That's . . . in a *car*crash . . . and that's it.
You know, you know, we're *sheltered* . . .
GLENNA. Who is?
EDMOND. You and I. White people. All of us. All of
us. We're doomed. The White Race is doomed. And do
you know *why.* . . ? Sit down . . .
GLENNA. I can't. I'm working.
EDMOND. And do you know *why*—you can do anything you *want* to do, you don't sit down because you're
working, the reason you don't sit down is you don't
want to sit down, because it's more comfortable to *ac-*

cept a law that questions it and live your life. All of us. *All* of us. We've bred the life out of ourselves. And we live in a fog. We live in a dream. Our life is a *school*house, and we're dead. (*pause*) How old are you?

GLENNA. Twenty-eight.

EDMOND. I've lived in a fog thirty-seven years. Most of the life I have to live. It's gone. It's gone. I wasted it. Because I didn't know. And you know what the answer is? To *live*. (*pause*) That's it. (*pause*) In one moment. In one moment. For which I thank God. (*pause*) To live. I want to tell you something. No one's ever going to know. Just you. That's it. No one is keeping score. And no one *cares* . . . (*pause*) It's our life. And that's all it is. Our only treasure is to act. I want to go home with you tonight.

GLENNA. Why?

EDMOND. Why do you think? I want to fuck you. (*pause*) It's as simple as that. What's your name?

GLENNA. Glenna. (*pause*) What's yours?

EDMOND. Edmond.

SCENE 16

GLENNA'S APARTMENT

EDMOND and GLENNA are lounging around semi-clothed. EDMOND shows GLENNA the survival knife.

EDMOND. You see this?

GLENNA. Yes.

EDMOND. That fucking nigger comes up to me, what am I fitted to do. He comes up, "Give me all your money." Thirty-seven years fits me to sweat and say he's underpaid, and he can't get a *job,* he's *bigger* than me . . . he's a killer, he don't care about his *life,* you understand, so he'd do anything. Eh? That's what I'm fitted to do. In a mess of intellectuality to wet my *pants* while this *coon* cuts my *dick* off . . . eh? Because I'm taught to *hate.* I want to tell you something. Something *spoke* to me, I gòt a *shock,* (I don't know, I got mad . . .) I got a *shock,* and I spoke *back* to him, that motherfucker, I came out there with my *knife,* and stuck it in his *neck,* eh? "Up your ass, you coon . . . you want to fight, *I'll* fight you, I'll cut out your fuckin' *heart,* eh, *I* don't give a fuck."

GLENNA. Yes.

EDMOND. Eh? I'm saying, *I* don't give a fuck, *I* got some warlike blood in *my* veins, too, you fucking spade, you coon. "The *blood* ran down his neck."

GLENNA. (*looking at knife*) With that?

EDMOND. You bet your ass.

GLENNA. Did you kill him?

EDMOND. Did I kill him?

GLENNA. Yes.

EDMOND. I don't care.

GLENNA. That's wonderful.

EDMOND. And in that moment . . . when I *spoke,* you understand, 'cause that was more important than the *knife,* when I spoke back to him, I DIDN'T FUCKING WANT TO *UNDERSTAND* . . . let *him* understand *me* . . . I wanted to KILL him. (*pause*) In that *moment* thirty years of prejudice came out of me. (*pause*) Thirty *years.* Of all those um um um of all those cleaning ladies . . .

GLENNA. Uh-huh . . .

EDMOND. . . . . uh? . . . who *might* have broke the **lamp. SO WHAT? You understand? For the first *time,***

I swear to god, for the first *time* I saw: THEY'RE PEO-
PLE, TOO.

GLENNA. (*pause*) Do you know who I hate?

EDMOND. Who is that?

GLENNA. Faggots.

EDMOND. Yes. I hate them, too. And you know why?

GLENNA. Why?

EDMOND. They suck cock. (*pause*) And that's the
truest thing you'll ever hear.

GLENNA. I hate them cause they don't like women.

EDMOND. They *hate* women.

GLENNA. I know that they do.

EDMOND. It makes you feel good to *say* it? Doesn't it?

GLENNA. Yes.

EDMOND. Then *say* it. *Say* it. If it makes you feel
whole. *Always* say it. *Always* for your*self* . . .

GLENNA. It's hard.

EDMOND. *Yes.*

GLENNA. Sometimes it's hard.

EDMOND. You're goddam right it's hard. And there's a
reason why it's hard?

GLENNA. Why?

EDMOND. So that we will stand up. So that we'll be
our*selves.* Glenna: (*pause*) . . . THERE IS NO *LAW*
. . . there is no *history* . . . there is just *now* . . . and if
there is a *God* he may love the weak, Glenna. (*pause*)
But he respects the strong. (*pause*) And if you are a *man*
you should be feared. (*pause*) You should be *feared*
. . . (*pause*) You must know you command respect.

GLENNA. That's why I love the Theatre . . .

EDMOND. Yes.

GLENNA. Because what you must ask respect for is
your*self* . . .

EDMOND. What do you mean?

GLENNA. When you're on stage.

EDMOND. Yes.

GLENNA. For *your* feelings.

EDMOND. Absolutely. Absolutely, yes . . .

GLENNA. And, and *not* be someone else.

EDMOND. Why should you . . .

GLENNA. . . . that's why, and I'm so proud to *be* in this profession . . .

EDMOND. . . . I don't blame you . . .

GLENNA. . . . because your aspirations . . .

EDMOND. . . . and I'll bet that you're good at it . . .

GLENNA. . . . they . . .

EDMOND. . . . they have no bounds

GLENNA. There's nothing . . .

EDMOND. . . . Yes. I understand . . .

GLENNA. To *bound* you but your soul.

EDMOND. (*pause*) Do something for me.

GLENNA. . . . uh . . .

EDMOND. *Act* something for me. Would you act something for me. . . ?

GLENNA. *Now?*

EDMOND. Yes.

GLENNA. Sitting right here. . . ?

EDMOND. Yes. (*pause*)

GLENNA. Would you really like me to?

EDMOND. You know I would. You see me sitting here, and you know that I would. I'd *love* it. Just because we both *want* to. I'd *love* you to. (*pause*)

GLENNA. What would you like me to do?

EDMOND. Whatever you'd like. What plays have you done?

GLENNA. Well, we've only done scenes.

EDMOND. You've only done scenes.

GLENNA. I shouldn't say "only." They contain the kernel of the play.

EDMOND. Uh-huh. (*pause*) What *plays* have you done?

GLENNA. In college I played Juliet.

EDMOND. In Shakespeare?

GLENNA. Yes. In Shakespeare. What do you think?

EDMOND. Well, I meant, there's *plays* named Juliet.

GLENNA. There are?

EDMOND. Yes.

GLENNA. I don't think so.

EDMOND. Well, there are. — Don't. Don't. Don't. Don't be so *limited*. And don't assume I'm dumb because I wear a suit and tie.

GLENNA. I don't assume that.

EDMOND. Because what we've *done* tonight. Since you met me, it didn't make a difference then. Forget it. All I meant, you say you are an actress . . .

GLENNA. I am an actress.

EDMOND. Yes. I say that's what you *say*. So *I* say what *plays* have you done. That's all.

GLENNA. The work I've done I have done for my peers.

EDMOND. What does that mean?

GLENNA. In class.

EDMOND. In class.

GLENNA. In class or workshop.

EDMOND. Not, not for a paying group.

GLENNA. No. Absolutely not.

EDMOND. Then you are not an actress. Face it. Let's start right. The two of us. I'm not lying to *you,* don't lie to *me*. And don't lie to yourself. *Face* it. You're a beautiful woman. You have *worlds* before you. I do, too.

Things to do. Things you can *discover.* What I'm saying, start *now,* start *tonight.* With *me. Be* with me. Be
what you *are.*

GLENNA. I am what I am.

EDMOND. That's absolutely right. And that's what I
loved when I saw you tonight. What I *loved.* I use that
word. (*pause*) I used that word. I loved a *woman.* Stand-
ing there. A working woman. Who brought life to what
she did. Who took a moment to *joke* with me. That's
. . . that's . . . that's . . . God *bless* you what you are.
Say it: I am a waitress. (*pause*) Say it.

GLENNA. What does it mean if I say something?

EDMOND. Say it with me. (*pause*)

GLENNA. What?

EDMOND. "I am a waitress."

GLENNA. I think that you better go.

EDMOND. If you want me to go I'll go. Say it with me.
Say what you are. And I'll say what *I* am.

GLENNA. . . . what *you* are . . .

EDMOND. I've *made* that discovery. Now: I want you
to change your life with me. Right now: for what*ever*
that we can be. *I* don't know what that is, *you* don't
know. Speak with me. Right now. Say it.

GLENNA. I don't know what you're talking about.

EDMOND. Oh, by the Lord, yes you do. Say it with
me. (*She takes out a vial of pills.*) What are those?

GLENNA. Pills.

EDMOND. For what? Don't take them.

GLENNA. I have this tendency to get anxious.

EDMOND. (*He knocks them from her hand.*) Don't
take them. Go *through* it. Go *through* with me.

GLENNA. You're scaring me.

EDMOND. I am not. I know when I'm scaring you.
*B*elieve me. (*pause*)

GLENNA. Get out. (*pause*)

EDMOND. Glenna. (*pause*)

GLENNA. Get out! GET OUT GET OUT! LEAVE ME THE FUCK ALONE!!! WHAT DID I DO, PLEDGE MY LIFE TO YOU? I LET YOU FUCK ME. GO AWAY.

EDMOND. Listen to me: you know what madness is?

GLENNA. I told you go away.

EDMOND. I'm lonely, too. I know what it is, too. Believe me. Do you know what madness is?

GLENNA. (*goes to phone, dials*) Susie. . . ?

EDMOND. It's self-indulgence.

GLENNA. Suse, can you come over here. . . ?

EDMOND. Will you please put that *down?* You know how *rare* this is. . . ? (*He knocks the phone out of her hands. GLENNA cowers.*)

GLENNA. Oh fuck . . .

EDMOND. Don't be ridiculous. I'm *talking* to you.

GLENNA. Don't hurt me. No. No. I can't deal with this.

EDMOND. Don't be ridic . . .

GLENNA. I . . . No. Help! Help.

EDMOND. . . . you're being . . .

GLENNA. . . . HELP!

EDMOND. . . . are you *insane?* What the fuck are you trying to *do,* for godsake?

GLENNA. Help!

EDMOND. You want to wake the *neighbors?*

GLENNA. WILL SOMEBODY HELP ME. . . ?

EDMOND. Shut up shut up!

GLENNA. Will somebody help you are the get *away* from me! You are the *devil.* I know who you are. I know what you want me to do. Get *away* from me. I curse *you,* you can't kill me, get away from me I'm good.

EDMOND. *WILL YOU SHUT THE FUCK UP?* You fucking *bitch.* You're *nuts* . . . (*He strikes her with the knife.*) Are you *insane?* Are you *insane* you fucking *idiot* . . . You stupid fucking *bitch* . . . You stupid fucking . . . *now* look what you've done. (*pause*) Now look what you've bloody fucking done.

SCENE 17

THE MISSION

EDMOND is attracted by the speech of a MISSION PREACHER. He walks to the front of the mission and listens outside the mission doors.

PREACHER. "Oh no, not me!" You say, "Oh no, not me. Not *me,* Lord, to whom you hold out your hand. Not *me* to whom you offer your eternal grace. Not *me* who can be saved." But *who* but you, I ask you? *Who* but you. You say you are a grievous sinner? He *knows* that you are. You say he does not know the *depth* of my iniquity. *Believe* me, friends, he does. And still you say, he does not know—you say this in your secret soul—he does not know the terrible depth of my unbelief. Believe me, friends, he knows that too. To *all* of you who say his grace is not meant to extend to one as black as you I say to WHO but you? To you *alone.* Not to the blessed. You think that Christ died for the blessed? That he died for the heavenly hosts? That did not make him God, my friends, it does not need a god to sacrifice for angels. It required a God to sacrifice for MAN. You hear me? For *you* . . . there is *none* so black but that he died for you. He died *especially* for you. Upon my life. On the graves of my family, and by the surety I have of his Eternal

Bliss HE DIED FOR YOU AND YOU ARE SAVED.
Praise *God,* my friends. Praise God and testify. Who
will come up and testify with me, my friends? (*pause*)

(*WOMAN from subway walks by. She sees EDMOND
and stares at him.*)

EDMOND. (*speaks up*) I will testify.
PREACHER. *Who* is that?
EDMOND. I will testify.
PREACHER. Sweet *God,* let that man come up here!
(*EDMOND starts into the Church.*)
WOMAN. (*shouts*) That's the Man! Someone! Call a
policeman! That's the man!
PREACHER. . . . who will come open up his soul?
Alleluia, my friends. *Be* with me.
WOMAN. That's the man. *Stop* him! (*EDMOND stops
and turns. He looks wonderingly at the WOMAN, then
starts inside.*)
POLICEMAN. Just a moment, sir.
EDMOND. I . . . I . . . I . . I . . . I'm on my way to
church.
PREACHER. Sweet *Jesus,* let that man come forth.
WOMAN. That's the man tried to rape me on the train.
(*The POLICEMAN closes the door to the Mission and
stands between EDMOND and the door.*) He had a
knife . . .
EDMOND. . . . there must be some mistake . . .
WOMAN. He tried to rape me on the train.
EDMOND. There's some mistake, I'm on my way to
church.
POLICEMAN. What's the trouble here?
EDMOND. No trouble, I'm on my way into the mis-
sion.

WOMAN. This man tried to rape me on the train yesterday.

EDMOND. Obviously the woman's mad.

POLICEMAN. Could I see some identification please?

EDMOND: Please, officer, I haven't time. I . . . I . . . it's been a long . . . I don't have my *wallet* on me. My name's Gregory Burke. I live at 428 22nd Street, I own the building. I . . . I have to go inside the Church.

POLICEMAN. You want to show me some. I.D.?

EDMOND. I don't have any. I told you.

POLICEMAN. You're going to have to come with me.

EDMOND. I . . . please . . . Yes. In one minute. Not . . . not now, I have to *preach*.

POLICEMAN. Come on.

EDMOND. You're making a . . . Please. Let me go. And I'll come with you afterward. I swear I will. I swear it on my life. There's been a mistake. I'm an elder in this church. Come *with* me if you will. I have to go and speak.

POLICEMAN. Look. (*Conciliatorily, he puts an arm on EDMOND. He feels something. He pulls back.*) What's that?

EDMOND. It's nothing. (*The POLICEMAN pulls out the survival knife.*) It's a knife. It's there for self-protection. (*The POLICEMAN throws EDMOND to the ground and handcuffs him.*)

SCENE 18

THE INTERROGATION

EDMOND and an INTERROGATOR at the Police Station.

INTERROGATOR. What was the knife for?

EDMOND. For protection.

INTERROGATOR. From whom?

EDMOND. Everyone.

INTERROGATOR. You know that it's illegal?

EDMOND. No.

INTERROGATOR. It is.

EDMOND. (*pause*) I'm sorry.

INTERROGATOR. Speaking to that woman in the way you did is construed as assault.

EDMOND. I never spoke to her.

INTERROGATOR. She identified you as the man who accosted her last evening on the subway.

EDMOND. She is seriously mistaken.

INTERROGATOR. If she presses charges you'll be arraigned for assault.

EDMOND. For *speaking* to her?

INTERROGATOR. You admit that you were speaking to her?

EDMOND. (*pause*) I want to ask you something. (*pause*)

INTERROGATOR. Alright.

EDMOND. Did you ever kick a dog? (*pause*) Well, that's what I did. Man to man. That's what I did. I made a simple, harmless comment to her, she responded like a fucking bitch.

INTERROGATOR. You trying to pick her up?

EDMOND. Why should I try to pick her up?

INTERROGATOR. She was an attractive woman.

EDMOND. She was *not* an attractive woman.

INTERROGATOR. You gay?

EDMOND. What business is that of yours?

INTERROGATOR. Are you?

EDMOND. NO.

INTERROGATOR. You married?

EDMOND. Yes IN fact. I was going back to my wife.

INTERROGATOR. You were going back to your wife?

EDMOND. I was going home to her.

INTERROGATOR. You said you were going back to her, what did you mean?

EDMOND. I'd left my wife, alright?

INTERROGATOR. You left your wife?

EDMOND. Yes.

INTERROGATOR. Why?

EDMOND. I was *bored.* Didn't that ever happen to *you?*

INTERROGATOR. And why did you lie to the officer?

EDMOND. What officer?

INTERROGATOR. Who picked you up. There's no Gregory Burke at the address you gave. You didn't give him your right name.

EDMOND. I was embarrassed.

INTERROGATOR. Why?

EDMOND. I didn't have my wallet.

INTERROGATOR. Why?

EDMOND. I'd left it at home.

INTERROGATOR. And why did that embarrass you?

EDMOND. I don't know. I have had no *sleep.* I just want to go *home.* I am a *solid* . . . look: my name is Edmond Burke, I live at 485 West Seventy-ninth Street. I work at Stearns and Harrington. I had a tiff with my wife. I went out on the town. I've learned my lesson. *Believe* me. I just want to go home. Whatever I've done I'll make right. (*pause*) Alright? (*pause*) Alright? These things happen and then they're done. When you *stopped* me I was going to church. I've been unwell. I'll confess to you that I've been confused but, but, . . . I've learned my lesson and I'm ready to go home.

INTERROGATOR. Why did you kill that girl?
EDMOND. What girl?
INTERROGATOR. That girl you killed.

SCENE 19

JAIL

*EDMOND's wife is visiting him. They sit across from
each other in silence for a while.*

EDMOND. How's everything?
WIFE. Fine. (*pause*)
EDMOND. I'm alright, too.
WIFE. Good. (*pause*)
EDMOND. You want to tell me that you're *mad* at me
or something?
WIFE. Did you kill that girl in her apartment?
EDMOND. Yes, but I want to tell you something . . . I
didn't mean to. But do you want to hear something *funny. . . ?* (now don't laugh . . .) I think I'd just had too
much coffee. (*pause*) I'll tell you something else: I think
that there are just too many people in the world. I think
that's why we kill each other. (*pause*) I . . . I . . . I suppose you're mad at me for leaving you. (*pause*) I don't
suppose you're, uh, inclined (or, nor do I think you
should be) to stand by me. I understand that. (*pause*)
I'm sure that there are marriages where the wife would.
Or the husband if it would go that way. (*pause*) But I
know ours is not one of that type. (*pause*) I know that
you wished at one point it would be. I wished that, too.
At one point. (*pause*) I know at certain times we wished

we could be . . . closer to each other. I can say that now. I'm sure this is the way you feel when someone near you dies. You never said the things you wanted desperately to say. It would have been so simple to say them. (*pause*) But you never did.

WIFE. You got the papers?

EDMOND. Yes.

WIFE. Good.

EDMOND. Oh, yes. I got them.

WIFE. Anything you need?

EDMOND. No. Can't think of a thing. (*The WIFE stands up, starts gathering her things together.*) You take care, now!

SCENE 20

THE NEW CELL

EDMOND is put in his new cell. His cellmate is a large, black PRISONER. EDMOND sits on his new bunk in silence a while.

EDMOND. You know, you know, you know, you know we can't distinguish between *anxiety* and *fear*. Do you know what I mean? I don't mean fear. I mean, I *do* mean "fear," I, don't mean *anxiety*. (*pause*) We, when we *fear* things I think that we *wish* for them. (*pause*) *Death.* Or "Burglars." (*pause*) Don't you think? We mean we *wish* they would come. Every fear hides a wish. Don't you think? (*pause*) I always knew that I would end up here. (*pause, to himself*) Every fear hides a wish. (*to his cellmate*) I think I'm going to like it here.

PRISONER. You do?

EDMOND. Yes, I do. Do you know why? It's simple. That's why I think that I am. You know, I always thought that *White* people should be in prison. I know it's the Black race we keep there. But I thought *we* should be there. You know why?

PRISONER. Why?

EDMOND. To be with the Black people. (*pause*) Does that sound too *simple* to you? (*pause*)

PRISONER. No.

EDMOND. Because we're *lonely*. (*pause*) But what I *know* . . . (*pause*) What I *know* I think that all this *fear,* this fucking *fear* we feel must hide a wish. Cause I don't feel it since I'm here. I *don't.* I think the first time in my life. (*pause*) In my whole adult life I don't feel fearful since I came in here. I think we are like birds. I think that humans are like birds. We suspect when there's going to be an *earthquake.* Birds know. They leave three days earlier. Something in their soul responds.

PRISONER. The birds leave when there's going to be an earthquake?

EDMOND. Yes. And I think, in our soul, *we, we* feel, we sense there is going to be . . .

PRISONER. Uh huh . . .

EDMOND. . . . a cataclysm. But we cannot flee. We're fearful. All the time. Because we can't trust what we know. That ringing. (*pause*) I think we feel. Some thing tells us "Get *out* of here." (*pause*) White people feel that. Do you feel that? (*pause*) Well. But I don't feel it since I'm here. (*pause*) I don't feel it since I'm here. I think I've settled. So, so, so I must be somewhere safe. Isn't that funny?

PRISONER. No.

EDMOND. You think it's not?

PRISONER. Yes.

EDMOND. Thank you.

PRISONER. Thass alright.

EDMOND. Huh. (*pause*)

PRISONER. You want a cigarette?

EDMOND. No, thank you. Not just now.

PRISONER. Thass alright.

EDMOND. Maybe later.

PRISONER. Sure. Now you know what?

EDMOND. What?

PRISONER. I think you just get on my body.

EDMOND. I, yes. What do you mean?

PRISONER. You should get on my body now.

EDMOND. I don't know what that means.

PRISONER. It means to suck my dick. (*pause*) Now don't you want to do that?

EDMOND. No.

PRISONER. Well, you jes do it anyway.

EDMOND. You're joking.

PRISONER. Not at all.

EDMOND. I don't think I could do that.

PRISONER. Well, you going to try or you going to die. Les get this out-the-way.

EDMOND. I, seriously . . . we're going to be here a long time and I don't think that we want to start like this.

PRISONER. I'm not no going to repeat myself.

EDMOND. I'll scream.

PRISONER. You *scream,* and you offend me. You are going to die. Look at me now and say I'm foolin'. (*pause*)

EDMOND. I . . . I . . . I . . . I . . . I can't, I can't do,
I . . . I

PRISONER. The mother*fuck* you can't. Right now,
missy. (*The PRISONER slaps EDMOND viciously
several times.*) *Right* now, Jim. An' you bes' be nice.

SCENE 21

THE CHAPLAIN

*EDMOND is sitting across from the Prison CHAP-
LAIN.*

CHAPLAIN. You don't have to talk.
EDMOND. I don't want to talk. (*pause*)
CHAPLAIN. Are you getting accustomed to life here?
EDMOND. Do you know what happened to me?
CHAPLAIN. No. (*pause*)
EDMOND. I was sodomized.
CHAPLAIN. Did you report it?
EDMOND. Yes.
CHAPLAIN. What did they say?
EDMOND. "That happens."
CHAPLAIN. I'm sorry it happened to you. (*pause*)
EDMOND. Thank you.
CHAPLAIN. (*pause*) Are you lonely?
EDMOND. Yes. (*pause*) Yes. (*pause*) I feel so
alone . . .
CHAPLAIN. Shhhh . . .
EDMOND. I'm so *empty* . . .
CHAPLAIN. Maybe you are ready to be *filled.*
EDMOND. That's *bullshit,* that's *bullshit.* That's pious
bullshit.

CHAPLAIN. Is it?

EDMOND. Yes.

CHAPLAIN. That you are ready to be filled? Is it impossible?

EDMOND. Yes. Yes. I don't know what's impossible.

CHAPLAIN. Nothing is impossible.

EDMOND. Oh. Nothing is impossible, Not to "God," is that what you're saying?

CHAPLAIN. Yes.

EDMOND. Well, then, you're full of *shit*. You understand that. If nothing's impossible to God, then let him let me walk *out* of here and be *free*. Let him cause a new *day*. In a perfect land full of *life*. And *Air*. Where people are *kind* to each other, and there's *work* to do. Where we grow up in *love,* and in security we're *wanted*. (*pause*) Let him do that. Let him. Tell him to do that. (*pause*) You *ass*hole—if nothing's impossible . . . I think *that* must be easy . . . Not: "Let me *fly*," or "If there is a God make him to make the sun come out at night." Go on. Please. Please. Please. I'm *begging* you. If you're so smart. Let him do that. (*pause*) Please. (*pause*) Please. I'm begging you.

CHAPLAIN. Are you sorry that you killed that girl? (*pause*) Edmond?

EDMOND. Yes. (*pause*)

CHAPLAIN. Are you sorry that you killed that girl?

EDMOND. I'm sorry about everything.

CHAPLAIN. But are you sorry that you killed? (*pause*)

EDMOND. Yes. (*pause*) Yes, I am. (*pause*) Yes.

CHAPLAIN. Why did you kill that girl?

EDMOND. I don't . . . I . . . I don't . . . (*pause*) I . . . (*pause*) I don't . . . (*pause*) I don't think . . . (*pause*) I . . . (*pause*) I don't . . . (*The CHAP-*

LAIN helps EDMOND up and leads him to the door.)

SCENE 22

ALONE IN THE CELL

EDMOND, alone in his cell, writes:

EDMOND. Dear Mrs. Brown. You don't remember me. Perhaps you do. Do you remember Eddie Burke who lived on Euclid? Maybe you do. I took Debbie to the Prom. I know that she never found me attractive, and I think, perhaps she was coerced in some way to go with me — though I can't think in what way. It also strikes me as I write that maybe she went of her own free will and I found it important to *think* that she went unwillingly. (*pause*) I don't think, however, this is true. (*pause*) She was a lovely girl. I'm sure if you remember me you will recall how taken I was with her then.

GUARD. You have a visitor.

EDMOND. Please tell them that I'm ill. (*GUARD exits. EDMOND gets up, stretches, goes to the window, looks out. To himself.*) What a day . . . (*He goes back to his table, sits down, yawns, picks up the paper.*)

SCENE 23

IN THE PRISON CELL

EDMOND and the PRISONER are each lying on their bunks.

EDMOND. You can't control what you make of your life.

PRISONER. Now, thass for *damn* sure.

EDMOND. There is a destiny that shapes our ends . . .

PRISONER. . . . uh huh . . .

EDMOND. Rough-hew them how we may.

PRISONER. How *e'er* we motherfucking may.

EDMOND. And that's the truth.

PRISONER. You *know* that is the truth.

EDMOND. . . . and people say that it's *heredity,* or it's environment . . . but, but I think it's something else.

PRISONER. What you think it is?

EDMOND. I think it's something *beyond* that.

PRISONER. Uh huh . . .

EDMOND. *Beyond* those things that we can know. (*pause*) I think maybe in dreams we see what it is. (*pause*) What do you think? (*pause*)

PRISONER. I don't know.

EDMOND. I don't think we *can* know. I think that if we *knew* it, we'd be dead.

PRISONER. We would be *God.*

EDMOND. We would be God. That's absolutely right.

PRISONER. Or, or some *genius.*

EDMOND. No, I don't think even *genius* could know what it is.

PRISONER. No, some great *genius,* (*pause*), or some *philosopher* . . .

EDMOND. I don't think even *genius* can see what we are.

PRISONER. You don't . . . *think* that . . . (*pause*)

EDMOND. I think that we can't perceive it.

PRISONER. *Something's* going on, I tell you *that.* I'm saying, *somewhere some* poor sucker knows what's happening.

EDMOND. Do you think?

PRISONER. *Shit* yes. Some whacked-out sucker. Somewhere. In the Ozarks? (*pause*) *Shit* yes. Some guy. (*pause*) Some inbred sucker, walks around all day . . . (*pause*)

EDMOND. You think?

PRISONER. Yeah. Maybe not *him* . . . but someone. (*pause*) Some fuck locked up, he's got time for reflection . . . (*pause*) Or some fuckin . . . I don't know, some *kid,* who's just been *born.* (*pause*)

EDMOND. Some kid that's just been born . . .

PRISONER. Yes. And you know, he's got no *preconceptions* . . .

EDMOND. Yes.

PRISONER. All he's got . . .

EDMOND. . . . that's absolutely right . . .

PRISONER. *Huh.* . . ?

EDMOND. Yes.

PRISONER. Is . . .

EDMOND. Maybe it's *memory* . . .

PRISONER. That's what I'm *saying.* That it just may *be* . . .

EDMOND. It could be.

PRISONER. Or . . .

EDMOND. . . . or some . . .

PRISONER. . . . some . . .

EDMOND. *Knowledge* . . .

PRISONER. . . . some . . .

EDMOND. . . . some in*tuition* . . .

PRISONER. Yes.

EDMOND. I don't even mean "intuition" . . . something . . . something . . .

PRISONER. Or some *animal* . . .

EDMOND. Why not. . . ?

PRISONER. That all the time we're saying we'll wait for the men from *space,* maybe they're *here* . . .

EDMOND. . . . maybe they are . . .

PRISONER . . . maybe they're *animals* . . .

EDMOND. Yes.

PRISONER. That were *leff* here . . .

EDMOND. *Aeons* ago.

PRISONER. *Long* ago . . .

EDMOND. . . . and have bred here . . .

PRISONER. Or maybe *we're* the animals . . .

EDMOND. . . . maybe we are . . .

PRISONER. *You* know, how they, *they* are supreme on their . . .

EDMOND. . . . yes.

PRISONER. On their *native* world . . .

EDMOND. But when you put them here.

PRISONER. *We* say they're only *dogs,* or *animals* and *scorn* them . . .

EDMOND. . . . yes.

PRISONER. We scorn them in our fear. But . . . don't you think. . . ?

EDMOND. . . . it very well could be . . .

PRISONER. But on their native *world* . . .

EDMOND. . . . uh huh . . .

PRISONER. They are *supreme* . . .

EDMOND. I think that's very . . .

PRISONER. An what *we* have done is to disgrace ourselves.

EDMOND. We have.

PRISONER. Because we did not treat them with respeck.

EDMOND. (*pause*) Maybe *we* were the animals.

PRISONER. Well, thass what I'm saying.

EDMOND. Maybe they're here to watch over us. Maybe

that's why they're here. Or to observe us. Maybe we're here to be punished. (*pause*) Do you think that there's a Hell?

PRISONER. I don't know. (*pause*)

EDMOND. I don't know. Do you think that we are there?

PRISONER. I don't know, man. (*pause*)

EDMOND. Do you think that we go somewhere when we die?

PRISONER. I don't know, man. I *like* to think so.

EDMOND. I do, too.

PRISONER. I sure would like to think so. (*pause*)

EDMOND. Perhaps it's Heaven.

PRISONER. (*pause*) I don't know.

EDMOND. I don't know either but perhaps it is. (*pause*)

PRISONER. I would like to think so.

EDMOND. I would, too. (*pause*) Goodnight. (*pause*)

PRISONER. Goodnight. (*EDMOND reaches up and gives the PRISONER a kiss, then he sits back on his bed.*)

END

FURNITURE PROPS

1 table
2 barstools
2 chairs
prison bunk (bottom removable)
large cardboard box
display case

SMALL AND HAND PROPS
1 large shoulder bag
2 wool blankets
1 briefcase
1 shopping bag
2 cups and saucers
serving tray
2 handbags
paper money
switchblade
survival knife
leaflets
pen and pen holder set
hotel registration cards
2 mugs
writing pad

COSTUMES

Edmond
three-piece suit
prison uniform
Fortune-teller
dark two-piece suit
Wife
light brown pants & sweater
rain coat
Man in bar
khaki pants & checkered jacket
Bartender
green pants & white shirt
Manager-male
dark polyester blue suit
B-girl
silver racing jacket, black pants
Peepshow girl
leotard
Card sharp
sweat pants & green fatigue jacket
Leafleteer
jeans, leather jacket, cap
Whorehouse manager-female
grey komali outfit
Whore
silk mini-skirt & low cut blouse
Hotel clerk
pin-striped pants & brown cardigan
Pawnshop clerk
brown polyester pants and shirt

Customer
brown corduroy jacket, green wool scarf
Woman on subway
tan trench-coat, skirt & blouse
Pimp
blue jeans & black jacket, shiny shoes
Glenna
black tuxedo pants & vest, pleated shirt
Cop
patrolman's uniform
Interrogater
grey suit, narrow tie, white shirt
Prisoner
grey prison uniform, slippers
Chaplain
black suit with white collar

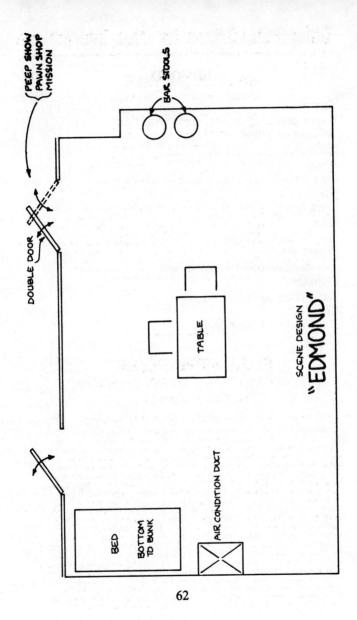

PEEP SHOW
PAWN SHOP
MISSION

BAR STOOLS

DOUBLE DOOR

TABLE

BED
BOTTOM
TO BUNK

AIR CONDITION DUCT

SCENE DESIGN
"EDMOND"

62

Other Publications for Your Interest

SPOILS OF WAR
(LITTLE THEATRE—DRAMA)
By MICHAEL WELLER

3 men, 3 women—Various Interior settings

Heretofore best known as the author of trenchant, bittersweet comedies such as *Loose Ends* and *Moonchildren*, as well as the screenplays for *Hair* and *Ragtime*, Mr. Weller is here in a deeper, more somber mode, as he chronicles the desperate attempts of a sixteen year-old boy to reconcile his divorced parents. Nobody writes better about disillusionment, about people whose hopes and dreams never quite lived up to reality. In *Moonchildren* and *Loose Ends* Mr. Weller dealt with how the Dream ended up in the sixties and seventies, respectively; here, the fuzzy decade of the fifties is explored through the eyes of Martin's parents, ex-thirties radicals who have chosen very different ways to cope with the changed, changing times. Elyse, the mother, is still a bohemian, a rebel without a cause who wants to live for something more than the rent and the price of hamburger, whereas Andrew, the father, has dropped back into the system, and accepted Life As It Is. And Martin is caught between these finally irreconcilable outlooks, unable to bring his parents back together and wondering what path *his* life will take. "Mr. Weller finds in one family's disintegration a paradigm of the postwar collapse of liberal idealism. This is without question Mr. Weller's most intelligent play, always intelligent and at times moving."—N.Y. Times. "Emotionally charged...a touching, lovely work."—N.Y. Post.

(#21294)

SPEED-THE-PLOW
(ADVANCED GROUPS—SERIOUS COMEDY)
By DAVID MAMET

2 men, 1 woman—Two interior. (may be simply suggested).

This is, without a doubt one of Mamet's best plays (including *American Buffalo* and the stunning, Pulitzer Prize-winning *Glengarry Glen Ross*). Joe Mantegna, Ron Silver and Madonna starred on Broadway in this hilarious and devastating satire of Hollywood, a microcosm of the macrocosm of American culture. Charlie Fox has discovered a terrific vehicle for a certain "hot" male movie star, and has brought it to his "best friend" Bobby Gould, "Head of Production" for a major film company. He coulda taken it across the street; but no, he's brought it to Bobby. Both see the script as their ticket to the really big table, where the real power is. The star wants to do it, and all they have to do is "pitch" it to their boss. The screenplay is a mass of typical action-picture cliches, which they have decided to pitch as a "buddy film"—the current "hot commodity". They'll be taking a meeting with the studio boss tomorrow; but tonight, Bobby has bet Charlie $500 that he can seduce Karen, a temp secretary. His ruse: he has given her a novel "by some Eastern sissy writer" which he has been asked to "courtesy-read" before saying thanks-but-no-thanks. Karen reads the novel and comes to Bobby's house that night—to convince him that *this*, and *not* the buddy film, should be the company's next project. Her arguments are convincing—all the more so when she agrees to sleep with Bobby, an experience which is apparently so transmogrifying that, much to Charlie's surprise, the next morning he finds he has to plead with Bobby not to put the buddy film "in turnaround", not to pitch the gloomy "sissy film". "By turns hilarious and chilling...[the] dialogue skyrockets."—N.Y. Times. Mamet's clearest, wittiest play."—N.Y. Daily News. "I laughed and laughed. The play is crammed with wonderful, dazzling, brilliant lines."—N.Y. Post. "There isn't a line that isn't somehow insanely funny or scarily insane."—Newsweek.

(#21281)

Other Publications for Your Interest

OTHER PEOPLE'S MONEY
(LITTLE THEATRE—DRAMA)

By JERRY STERNER

3 men, 2 women—One Set

Wall Street takeover artist Lawrence Garfinkle's intrepid computer is going "tilt" over the undervalued stock of New England Wire & Cable. He goes after the vulnerable company, buying up its stock to try and take over the company at the annual meeting. If the stockholders back Garfinkle, they will make a bundle—but what of the 1200 employees? What of the local community? Too bad, says Garfinkle, who would then liquidate the company—take the money and run. Set against the charmingly rapacious financier are Jorgenson, who has run the company since the Year One and his chief operations officer, Coles, who understands, unlike the genial Jorgenson, what a threat Garfinkle poses to the firm. They bring in Kate, a bright young woman lawyer, who specializes in fending off takeovers—and who is the daughter of Jorgenson's administrative assistant, Bea. Kate must not only contend with Garfinkle—she must also move Jorgenson into taking decisive action. Should they use "greenmail"? Try to find a "White Knight"? Employ a "shark repellent"? This compelling drama about Main Street vs. Wall Street is as topical and fresh as today's headlines, giving its audience an inside look at what's *really going on* in this country and asking trenchant questions, not the least of which is whether a corporate raider is really the creature from the Black Lagoon of capitalism or the Ultimate Realist come to save business from itself.

(#17064)

THE DOWNSIDE
(LITTLE THEATRE—COMEDY)

By RICHARD DRESSER

6 men, 2 women—Combination Interior

These days, American business is a prime target for satire, and no recent play has cut as deep, with more hilarious results, than this superb new comedy from the Long Wharf Theatre, Mark & Maxwell, a New Jersey pharmaceuticals firm, has acquired U.S. rights to market an anti-stress drug manufactured in Europe, pending F.D.A. approval; but the marketing executives have got to come up with a snazzy ad campaign by January—and here we are in December! The irony is that nowhere is this drug more needed than right there at Mark & Maxwell, a textbook example of corporate ineptitude, where it seems all you have to do to get ahead is look good in a suit. The marketing strategy meetings get more and more pointless and frenetic as the deadline approaches. These meetings are "chaired" by Dave, the boss, who is never actually there—he is a voice coming out of a box, as Dave phones in while jetting to one meeting or another, eventually directing the ad campaign on his mobile phone while his plane is being hijacked! Doesn't matter to Dave, though—what matters is the possible "downside" of this new drug: hallucinations. "Ridiculous", says the senior marketing executive Alan: who then proceeds to tell how Richard Nixon comes to his house in the middle of the night to visit..."Richard Dresser's deft satirical sword pinks the corporate image repeatedly, leaving the audience amused but thoughtful."—Meriden Record. "Funny and ruthlessly cynical."—Phila. Inquirer. "A new comedy that is sheer delight."—Westport News. "The Long Wharf audience laughed a lot, particularly those with office training. But they were also given something to ponder about the way we get things done in America these days, or rather pretend to get things done. No wonder the Japanese are winning."—L.A. Times.

(#6718)

Edmond

A DRAMA

by David Mamet

Samuel French, Inc.

Also by DAVID MAMET.......

AMERICAN BUFFALO
THE CHERRY ORCHARD (translation)
DARK PONY
A Collection of DRAMATIC SKETCHES &
    MONOLOGUES
THE DUCK VARIATIONS
GLENGARRY GLEN ROSS
LAKEBOAT
A LIFE IN THE THEATRE
MR. HAPPINESS
THE POET AND THE RENT
REUNION
THE SANCTITY OF MARRIAGE
SEXUAL PERVERSITY IN CHICAGO
THE SHAWL
SPEED-THE-PLOW
THREE JEWISH PLAYS
UNCLE VANYA (translation)
THE WATER ENGINE
THE WOODS

Consult our *Basic Catalogue of Plays* for details.

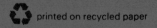